Down the Columbia

by A. K. Marina
illustrated by Bob Novak

 HOUGHTON MIFFLIN HARCOURT
School Publishers

Printed in China

ISBN-13: 978-0-547-02593-3
ISBN-10: 0-547-02593-9

8 9 10 0940 18 17 16 15 14 13
4500416971

"Do you hear it?" Pa asked excitedly.

Minnie listened and nodded yes. The river sounded like a herd of horses stampeding in the distance. The roar made her heart beat fast. It made her shudder.

"We must be close," Ma said.

"Very close," Pa responded.

Then they saw it—the wide, dark blue river. Water surged against sharp rocks on the river's edge, spraying white foam into the air. Ripples moved quickly across the water's surface. Minnie had never seen anything like it. *How will we ever get down this river?* Minnie thought.

Minnie's family had finally reached the Columbia River. For five long months, they had been traveling on the Oregon Trail. Like other adventurous Americans, they had sold most of their belongings, bought a wagon, and headed west from St. Louis, Missouri. They were going to Oregon City, where Pa would work for a lumber company. They would build a new house and start a new life.

Reaching the river meant that Oregon City was very close. Soon, Minnie hoped, the long days on the trail would be over. But before that could happen, the family faced the hardest part of their journey.

The trail stopped where the Cascade Mountain Range crossed the river. No one had figured out an easy way through the Cascades. So, to continue west, pioneers were forced to go down the Columbia River.

Minnie and her parents see the daunting Columbia River for the first time.

3

"Impossible!" Minnie blurted out as her parents talked about going down the river.

"There's always a way. You should know that by now," Pa said. Pa was constantly telling Minnie to never give up and to keep looking for solutions.

In the village, Pa spoke to a ferry operator who owned a large raft. The raft could carry two wagons down the river. Pa looked shocked and then angry as he talked to the ferry operator. Finally, shaking his head, Pa walked slowly back to Ma and Minnie.

Pa speaks with a ferry operator.

"What a scoundrel," Pa muttered. "Guess how much he would charge to take us downriver?"

"Twenty dollars?" Ma asked anxiously.

"Eighty!" Pa exclaimed.

"*Eighty dollars!*" Ma nearly yelled. "Why, that's more than what our wagon cost!"

The ferry operator knew that people traveling to Oregon City had only two choices—go on his raft or don't go at all. He was

The cost of the ferry trip surprises Ma.

taking advantage of pioneers who were tired after their months-long journey along the trail. Because the pioneers needed to go down the river, there was nothing they could do but pay whatever the ferry operator asked.

Ma and Pa discuss how to get to Oregon City.

Ma took out the metal box that held the family's life savings. She counted the money. Even if they had wanted to, there wasn't enough to pay the ferry operator.

That night, Ma and Pa discussed their options. Pa said they could cut down pine trees and build their own raft.

"The river is so dangerous," said Ma. "And we've never built a raft before. That's a big disadvantage. And if we don't build it right, we'll be in trouble."

"Some folks say that there are new land trails to Oregon City," Ma suggested. But Pa balked at the idea. He said that very few people had been on those trails. He'd heard they might be unsafe.

"Some people hire the Indians around here to take them down the river," Pa said. "But we can't afford that either."

Ma and Pa had <mark>lectured</mark> Minnie about staying away from Indians, but Minnie didn't share her parents' fear. After all, Minnie thought, she and her parents had traveled hundreds of miles and had witnessed many disasters. They had seen people injured by frightened oxen. They had watched wagons slide down muddy hillsides and topple over. They had seen people become deathly ill from spoiled food and bad water. But in all their travels, they had never met anyone who'd had a <mark>mishap</mark> with an Indian.

Minnie recalls a disaster she saw on the trail.

In the morning, Minnie took a walk along a small stream, feeling worried. Ma and Pa were still discussing how to get to Oregon City. Ma and Pa had found a way to get around every problem they had faced on the journey. But this problem was different.

Minnie was lost in her thoughts. Suddenly, she heard people speaking an unfamiliar language. An Indian woman and boy were on the other side of the stream. They were picking blackberries. Minnie quickly ducked behind a large tree. She thought about Pa and Ma's warning to stay away from Indians. Luckily, the woman and boy hadn't noticed her.

Minnie hides.

The boy jumps from rock to rock in the stream.

The woman worked steadily, plucking ripe berries from the bushes. But the boy seemed less interested in the work. After picking a few berries, he began jumping from rock to rock in the stream.

I should turn around and slip into the forest, Minnie thought. Suddenly, there was a splash nearby. The boy had lost his footing and slipped into the stream. Minnie saw him fall forward. His head struck a large rock, and he landed facedown and motionless in the water.

Minnie looked from the boy to the woman. She was so intent on her work that she hadn't noticed the boy's fall. Minnie looked back to the boy, who still wasn't moving.

What should I do? wondered Minnie. The boy was hurt. He might drown. But Ma and Pa had told her to never speak to Indians.

Yet, Minnie knew this was a matter of life or death. She had to act. Minnie stepped out from behind the tree and toward the boy. She shouted, "Help!" Then she rushed to the boy and lifted his head out of the water.

Minnie rescues the boy.

Seconds later, the woman was at Minnie's side. Together, they pulled the boy to the shore. They laid him on his back. Minnie could see a gash and bruise on his forehead.

The woman quickly bent over the boy and listened for his breathing. Suddenly and violently, he coughed, turned on his side, and spit out a mouthful of water. The woman's face turned from a look of horror to one of relief.

As the boy sat up, the woman turned to Minnie. Her face was filled with gratitude.

"Is he all right?" Minnie asked, motioning to the boy.

The woman did not respond, but she continued to smile at Minnie.

"I'm... I'm all right," stammered the boy.

Minnie was startled. He spoke English!

After a few minutes, the boy recovered enough to talk some more. He and Minnie exchanged stories. He told her about his family's tribe, who lived near the river. She told him about her family's trip and the obstacle they now faced.

The boy turned to his mother and spoke in their native language. Then, he turned back to Minnie. "You saved my life. Now, I want to help you."

He told Minnie to get her parents. So Minnie ran back to camp.

"Where were you?" Pa asked.

"Well, I met some folks. Some Indians," Minnie said softly.

Minnie runs back to camp.

"What?" Ma exclaimed.

Minnie quickly explained what had happened. "I helped them, and so they want to help us. I trust them. Please."

"Minnie, we don't know them," Ma said worriedly.

Pa sighed and stood up. "Let's go and meet them," he said. "This might be the only chance we have."

An Indian man stood with the woman and the boy. He held out his hand. Minnie was happy when Pa shook it. The Indian family had a canoe. They were going to Oregon City to trade salmon for supplies. The  family knew the parts of the river that were dangerous. It would be safe to go with them.

"You can join us," the Indian boy said. "But you will have to leave your wagon behind."

The wagon was their most valuable possession. But Pa and Ma were willing to leave it behind to get to Oregon City.

"Your father is a generous man," Pa said. "Tell him that we will come."

The next day, Ma, Pa, and Minnie packed their belongings into a trunk. They carried the trunk to the Indians' long canoe. The canoe was an amazing boat. When Minnie stepped into it, it didn't rock from side to side. It was sturdy.

After everyone was in the canoe, Pa smiled at Minnie. "You kept looking for a solution, and you found one!" he said.

Their adventure on the Columbia River was about to begin.

Minnie and her family paddle down the Columbia River toward Oregon City.

Responding

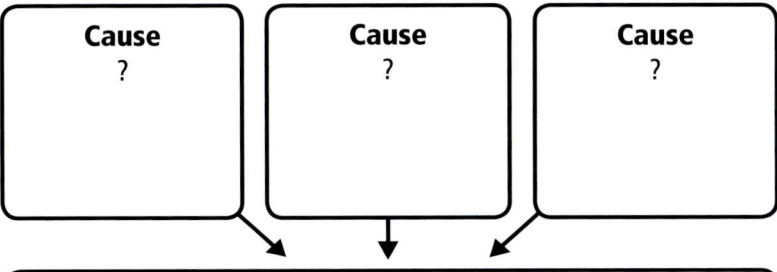

✓ **TARGET SKILL** **Cause and Effect** What causes Pa to leave the family's wagon behind before reaching Oregon City? Copy and complete the chart below.

Cause ?	Cause ?	Cause ?

Effect
Pa is willing to abandon the family's wagon before reaching Oregon City.

✏️ Write About It

Text to World Pioneers faced many challenges during the long trip west. Think of some of the challenges faced by pioneers. Write a paragraph describing one challenge. What were the causes of this challenge? What were the effects of this challenge?

✓ TARGET VOCABULARY

balked	mishap
beacon	quaking
disadvantage	rustling
fared	surged
lectured	torment

✓ **TARGET SKILL** **Cause and Effect** Tell how events are related and how one event causes another.

✓ **TARGET STRATEGY** **Analyze/Evaluate** Think carefully about the text and form an opinion about it.

GENRE **Historical Fiction** is a story whose characters and events are set in a real period of history.